JOHN DENVER
& THE MUPPETS:
A CHRISTMAS TOGETHER

Arranged and Edited by

Milton Okun

Concept by Jim Henson and John Denver

THE MUPPET PERFORMERS
FRANK OZ as Miss Piggy, Fozzie Bear and Animal
JERRY NELSON as Robin, Floyd and Lew Zealand
RICHARD HUNT as Scooter, Janice, Statler and Beaker
DAVE GOELZ as The Great Gonzo, Zoot, Beauregard and Dr. Bunsen Honeydew
AND
JIM HENSON as Kermit the Frog, Rowlf, Waldorf and Dr. Teeth
WITH
LOUISE GOLD, KATHRYN MULLEN, STEVE WHITMIRE

Associate Music Editor — Dan Fox
Art Director: Album — Michael K. Frith
Art Director: Folio — Gil Gjersvik
Album Photography: Nancy Moran/Donal Holway

ISBN 978-1-57560-558-6

The Twelve Days of Christmas

Traditional English Carol
Arranged by Milton Okun

sixth day of Christ - mas my true love gave to me six geese a - laying,
seventh day of Christ - mas my true love gave to me sev - en swans a swim-ming,
eighth day of Christ - mas my true love gave to me eight maids a - milk-ing,
ninth day of Christ - mas mi mi mi mi mi mi nine la - dies danc-ing,
tenth day of Christ - mas my true love gave to me ten Lords a leap-ing,
- leventh day of Christ - mas my true love gave to me e- - lev- en pip-ers pip-ing,
twelfth day of Christ - mas my true love gave to me twelve drum-mers drum-ming,

five gold _____ rings (bu - dum bum bum) four ___ call - ing birds,
(from the 9th day)

three French hens, two ___ tur - tle doves and a part - ridge ___ in a pear

tree. _____ On the (e -)

D.S. six times
last time
to Coda

tree. _____

The Peace Carol

Words and Music by
Bob Beers

Christmas Is Coming

Traditional English Carol
Arranged by Milton Okun

(Round)

A Baby Just Like You

Words and Music by
John Denver and Joe Henry

Deck the Halls

Traditional Welsh Carol
Arranged by Milton Okun

When the River Meets the Sea

Words and Music by
Paul Williams

Little Saint Nick

Words and Music by
Brian Wilson and Mike Love

Noel: Christmas Eve, 1913

Lyric by Robert Bridges

Music by Lee Holdridge

*Guitarists: Chords are played finger style.

Have Yourself a Merry Little Christmas

Words and Music by
Hugh Martin and Ralph Blane

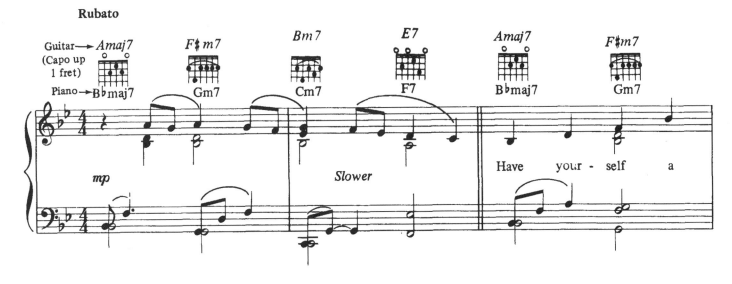

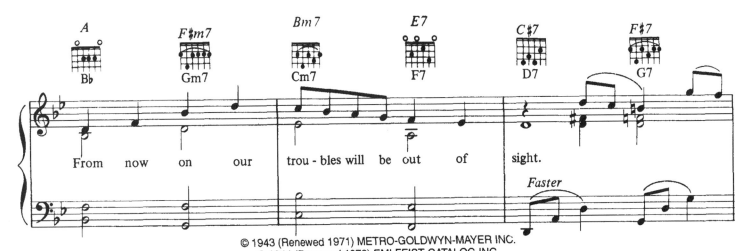

31

THE TWELVE DAYS OF CHRISTMAS

Traditional English Carol

On the first day of Christmas my true love gave to me
A partridge in a pear tree.

On the second day of Christmas my true love gave to me
Two turtle doves
And a partridge in a pear tree.

On the third day of Christmas my true love gave to me
Three french hens
Two turtle doves
And a partridge in a pear tree.

On the fifth day of Christmas my true love gave to me
Four calling birds
Three French hens
Two turtle doves
And a partridge in a pear tree.

On the sixth
On the seventh
On the eighth
On the ninth   } *day of Christmas my true love gave to me*
On the tenth
On the eleventh
On the twelfth

Six geese a-laying
Seven swans a-swimming
Eight maids a-milking
Nine ladies dancing   } *Five gold rings*
Ten lords a-leaping
Eleven pipers piping
Twelve drummers drumming

Four calling birds
Three French hens
Two turtle doves
And a partridge in a pear tree.

THE PEACE CAROL

Words and Music by Bob Beers

The garment of life be it tattered and torn,
The cloak of the soldier is weathered and worn,
But what child is this that was poverty born,
The peace of Christmas Day.

The branch that bears the bright holly,
The dove that rests in yonder tree,
The light that shines for all to see,
The peace of Christmas Day.

The branch that bears the bright holly,
The dove that rests in yonder tree,
The light that shines for all to see,
The peace of Christmas Day.

The hope that has slumbered for two thousand years,
A promise that silenced a thousand fears,
A faith that can hobble an ocean of tears,
The peace of Christmas Day.

The branch that bears the bright holly,
The dove that rests in yonder tree,
The light that shines for all to see,
The peace of Christmas Day.

Add all the grief that people may bear,
Total the strife and the trouble and care,
Put them in columns, then leave them right there,
The peace of Christmas Day.

The branch that bears the bright holly,
The dove that rests in yonder tree,
The light that shines for all to see,
The peace of Christmas Day.
(Repeat)

CHRISTMAS IS COMING (Round)

Traditional English Carol

Christmas is coming, the goose is getting fat;
Please to put a penny in the old man's hat.
If you haven't got a penny a ha' penny will do;
If you haven't got a ha' penny, then God bless you.

A BABY JUST LIKE YOU

Words and Music by John Denver and Joe Henry

The season is upon us now, a time for gifts and giving,
And as the year draws to its close, I think about my living:
The Christmas time when I was young, the magic and the wonder,
But colors dull and candles dim, and dark my standing under.
Oh, little angel, shining light, you've set my soul to dreaming.
You've given back my joy in life and filled me with new meaning.

A savior King was born that day, a baby just like you,
And as the wise men came with gifts, I've come with my gift too:
That peace on earth fills up your time, that brotherhood surrounds you,
That you may know the warmth of love and wrap it all around you.

It's just a wish, a dream I'm told, from days when I was young.
Merry Christmas, little _ _ _ _ _ _ _ ,
Merry Christmas, everyone!
Merry Christmas, little _ _ _ _ _ _ _ ,
Merry Christmas, everyone.

DECK THE HALLS

Traditional Welsh Carol

Deck the halls with boughs of holly,
Fa la la la la la la la la.
Tis the season to be jolly,
Fa la la la la la la la la.
Don we now our gay apparel,
Fa la la la la la la la la.
Troll the ancient Yuletide carol,
Fa la la la la la la la la.

See the blazing Yule before us,
Fa la la la la la la la la.
Strike the harp and join the chorus,
Fa la la la la la la la la.
Follow me in merry measure,
Fa la la la la la la la la.
While I tell of Yuletide treasure,
Fa la la la la la la la la.

Fast away the old year passes,
Fa la la la la la la la la.
Hail the new ye lads and lasses,
Fa la la la la la la la.
Sing we joyous all together,
Fa la la la la la la la la.
Heedless of the wind and weather,
Fa la la la la la la la la.
Fa la la la la la la la la.

WHEN THE RIVER MEETS THE SEA

Words and Music by Paul Williams

When the mountain touches the valley, all the clouds are taught to fly;
Thus our souls will leave this land most peacefully.
Tho' our minds be filled with questions, in our hearts we'll understand,
When the river meets the sea.

Like a flower that has blossomed in the dry and barren sand,
We are born and born again most gracefully.
Thus the winds of time will take us with a sure and steady hand.
When the river meets the sea.

Patience my brothers and patience my son;
In that sweet and final hour truth and justice will be done.
Like a baby when it is sleeping in its loving mother's arms,
What a newborn baby dreams is a mystery. (A mystery)
But his life will find a purpose and in time he'll understand,
When the river meets the sea,
When the river meets the almighty sea.

LITTLE SAINT NICK

Words and Music by Brian Wilson and Mike Love

Oo, Merry Christmas Santa.
Christmas comes this time each year.

Well, way up north where the air gets cold,
There's a tale about Christmas that you've all been told.
And a real famous cat all dressed up in red,
And he spends his whole year working out in his sled.
It's the Little Saint Nick (Little Saint Nick),
It's the Little Saint Nick (Little Saint Nick).

Just a little bobsled we call it Old Saint Nick,
But she'll walk the toboggan with a four-speed stick;
She's candy-apple red with a ski for a wheel.
And when Santa gives the gas, man just watch her peel.
It's the Little Saint Nick (Little Saint Nick)

Run, run reindeer,
Run, run, reindeer,
Run, run, reindeer,
Run, run, reindeer,
Run, run, run, yeah.

He's haulin' through the snow at a fright'nin' speed,
With a half dozen deer, with Rudy to lead.
He's got to wear goggles cuz the snow really flies,
And he's cruisin' ev'ry pad with a little surprise.
It's the Little Saint Nick (Little Saint Nick),
It's the Little Saint Nick (Little Saint Nick).

Oo, Merry Christmas Saint Nick.
Run, run, run, yeah etc.
(Repeat)
Oo, Merry Christmas Saint Nick.

HAVE YOURSELF A MERRY LITTLE CHRISTMAS

Words and Music by Henry Martin and Ralph Blane

Have yourself a Merry little Christmas,
Let your heart be light;
From now on our troubles will be out of sight.
Have yourself a Merry little Christmas,
Make the Yuletide gay;
From now on our troubles will be miles away.

Here we are as in olden days,
Happy golden days of yore.
Faithful friends who are dear to us,
Gather near to us once more.

Thru the years we all will be together,
If the fates allow;
Hang a shining star upon the highest bough,
And have yourself a Merry little Christmas now.

NOEL: CHRISTMAS EVE 1913

Lyric by Robert Bridges Music by Lee Holdrige

A frosty Christmas eve when the stars were shining,
I travell'd forth alone where westward falls the hill.
And from many, many a village in the darkness of the valley,
Distant music reached me, peals of bells were ringing.

Then sped my thoughts to olden times, to that first of Christmas'
When the shepherds who were watching heard music in the fields.
And they sat there and they marvel'd and they knew they could not tell,
Whether it were angels or the bright stars a-singing.

But to me heard afar it was starry music,
The singing of the angels, the comfort of our Lord.
Words of old that come a-trav'ling by the riches of the times,
And I softly listened, as I stood upon the hill,
And I softly listened, as I stood upon the hill.

THE CHRISTMAS WISH

Words and Music by Danny Allen Wheetman

I don't know if you believe in Christmas,
Or if you have presents underneath the Christmas tree,
But if you believe in love, that will be more than enough,
For you to come and celebrate with me.

For I have held the precious gift that love brings,
Even though I never saw a Christmas star.
I know there is a light, I have felt it burn inside,
And I have seen it shining from afar.

Christmas is the time to come together,
A time to put all diff'rences aside.
And I reach out my hand to the family of man,
To share the joy I feel at Christmas time.

For the truth that binds us all together,
I would like to say a simple prayer;
That at this special time, you will have true peace of mind,
And love to last throughout the coming year.

And if you believe in love,
That will be more than enough,
For peace to last throughout the coming year,
And peace on earth will last throughout the year.

SILENT NIGHT, HOLY NIGHT

Mohr, Gruber

Stille nacht, Heilige nacht!
Alles schlaft, einsam wacht,
Nur das traute, hoch heilige Paar,
Holder Knabe im lockigen Haar,
Schlaf' im himmlischer Ruh',
Schlaf' im himmlischer Ruh'.

Silent night, Holy night,
All is calm, all is bright,
Round yon Virgin, Mother and Child,
Holy Infant so tender and mild,
Sleep in heavenly peace,
Sleep in heavenly peace.

WE WISH YOU A MERRY CHRISTMAS

Traditional English Folksong

(Chorus)
We wish you a Merry Christmas,
We wish you a Merry Christmas,
We wish you a Merry Christmas,
And a Happy New Year.

Now bring us some figgy pudding,
Now bring us some figgy pudding,
Now bring us some figgy pudding,
And bring some out here.

(Repeat Chorus)
We won't go until we get some,
We won't go until we get some,
We won't go until we get some,
So bring some out here.

(Repeat Chorus)
We wish you a Merry Christmas,
We wish you a Merry Christmas,
We wish you a Merry Christmas,
And a Happy New Year.

The Christmas Wish

Words and Music by
Danny Allen Wheetman

neath   the Christ-mas   tree,___
star. _____
prayer; _____

But if you   be -
I know   there
That at   this

lieve   in love___
is   a light,___
spe - cial time___

that will be   more
I have felt   it
you will have   true

than e - nough
burn in - side,
peace of mind

For
And
And

you   to come and
I   have seen   it
love   to last   through

cel - e - brate___   with
shin - ing_____ from a -

me.
far.

Christ - mas is   the

time to come to-geth-er, A time to put all

dif-f'ren-ces a - side. And I reach

out my hand to the fam - i - ly of man To share the joy I

feel at Christ - mas time.

D.S. al Coda

44

out   the   com - ing   year.

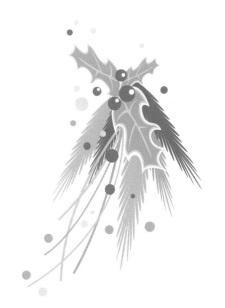

ALFIE, THE CHRISTMAS TREE

Words and Music by John Denver

Did you ever hear the story of the Christmas tree
Who just didn't want to change the show?
He liked living in the woods and playing with squirrels;
He liked icicles and snow;
He liked wolves and eagles and grizzly bears
And critters and creatures that crawled.
Why, bugs were some of his very best friends,
Spiders and ants and all.

Now, that's not to say that he never looked down
On the vision of twinkling lights;
Or on mirrored bubbles and peppermint canes
And a thousand other delights.
And he often had dreams of tiny reindeer
And a jolly old man in a sleigh
Full of toys and presents and wonderful things,
And the story of Christmas Day.

Oh, Alfie believed in Christmas all right.
He was full of Christmas cheer
All of each and every day
And all throughout the year.
To him it was more than a special time,
Much more than a special day.
It was more than a beautiful story;
It was a special kind of way.

You see, some folks have never heard a jingle bell ring
And they've never heard of Santa Claus.
They've never heard the story of the Son of God;
And that made Alfie pause.
Did that mean that they'd never know of peace on earth?
Or the brotherhood of man?
Or know how to love, or know how to give?
If they can't, no one can.

You see, life is a very special kind of thing,
Not just for a chosen few;
But for each and every living, breathing thing,
Not just for me and you.
So in your Christmas prayers this year,
Alfie asked me if I'd ask you
To say a prayer for the wind, and the water and the wood,
And those who live there too!

Carol for a Christmas Tree

Music by
Lee Holdridge

Silent Night, Holy Night

Words by Joseph Mohr

Music by Franz Gruber
Arranged by Milton Okun

We Wish You a Merry Christmas

Traditional English Folksong
Arranged by Milton Okun

*Note: Guitarists play chords finger style

More Great Piano/Vocal Books

FROM CHERRY LANE

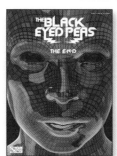

For a complete listing of Cherry Lane titles available,
including contents listings, please visit our web site at
www.cherrylane.com

See your local music dealer or contact:

7777 W. BLUEMOUND RD. P.O. BOX 13819 MILWAUKEE, WI 53213

Prices, contents and availability subject to change without notice.

Cherry Lane Music is your source for
JOHN DENVER SONGBOOKS!

PIANO/VOCAL BOOKS

JOHN DENVER ANTHOLOGY
A collection of 54 of this music legend's greatest tunes, including: Annie's Song • Follow Me • Leaving on a Jet Plane • Rocky Mountain High • Sunshine on My Shoulders • and more, plus a biography and John's reflections on his many memorable songs.
02502165 Piano/Vocal/Guitar $22.95

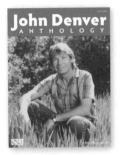

JOHN DENVER ANTHOLOGY
Easy arrangements of 34 of the finest from this beloved artist. Includes: Follow Me • Grandma's Feather Bed • Leaving on a Jet Plane • Matthew • Perhaps Love • Rocky Mountain High • Sunshine on My Shoulders • Thank God I'm a Country Boy • and many more.
02501366 Easy Piano $19.99

THE BEST OF JOHN DENVER – EASY PIANO
A collection of 18 Denver classics arranged for easy piano. Contains: Leaving on a Jet Plane • Take Me Home, Country Roads • Rocky Mountain High • Follow Me • and more.
02505512 Easy Piano $9.95

THE BEST OF JOHN DENVER – PIANO SOLOS
Best of John Denver – Piano Solos is a fabulous collection of 10 greatest hits from the legendary country artist. It includes many of his major hits including: Annie's Song • Leaving on a Jet Plane • Rocky Mountain High • and Take Me Home, Country Roads.
02503629 Piano Solo $10.95

A JOHN DENVER CHRISTMAS
A delightful collection of Christmas songs and carols recorded by John Denver. Includes traditional carols (Deck the Halls • Hark! The Herald Angels Sing • The Twelve Days of Christmas) as well as such contemporary songs as: A Baby Just Like You • Christmas for Cowboys • Christmas Like a Lullaby • and The Peace Carol.
02500002 Piano/Vocal/Guitar $14.95

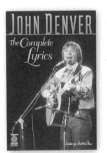

JOHN DENVER: THE COMPLETE LYRICS
An extremely gifted singer/songwriter, John Denver possessed the unique ability to marry melodic music with gentle, thought-provoking words that endeared him to his countless fans. Now, for the first time ever, John Denver's lyrics have been printed in their entirety: no other book like this exists! It contains lyrics to more than 200 songs, and includes an annotated discography showing all the songs, and an index of first lines. This collection also features an introduction by Tom Paxton, and a foreword from Milt Okun, John Denver's first record producer, and the founder of Cherry Lane Music.
02500459 .... $16.95

JOHN DENVER'S GREATEST HITS
This collection combines all of the songs from Denver's three best-selling greatest hits albums. 34 songs in all, including: Leaving on a Jet Plane • For Baby (For Bobbie) • Thank God I'm a Country Boy • Annie's Song • Perhaps Love • I Want to Live.
02502166 Piano/Vocal/Guitar $17.95

JOHN DENVER – A LEGACY OF SONG
This collection celebrates one of the world's most popular and prolific entertainers. Features 25 of John's best-loved songs with his commentary on each: Annie's Song • Fly Away • Leaving on a Jet Plane • Rocky Mountain High • Sunshine on My Shoulders • Take Me Home, Country Roads • Thank God I'm a Country Boy • and more, plus a biography, discography, reflections on John's numerous accomplishments, and photos spanning his entire career.
02502151 Piano/Vocal/Guitar Softcover $24.95

JOHN DENVER & THE MUPPETS – A CHRISTMAS TOGETHER
Back by popular demand! This book featuring John Denver, Kermit, and all the Muppets includes 12 holiday songs: A Baby Just like You • Carol for a Christmas Tree • Christmas Is Coming • The Christmas Wish • Deck the Halls • Have Yourself a Merry Little Christmas • Little Saint Nick • Noel: Christmas Eve, 1913 • The Peace Carol • Silent Night, Holy Night • The Twelve Days of Christmas • We Wish You a Merry Christmas.
02500501 Piano/Vocal/Guitar $9.95

POEMS, PRAYERS AND PROMISES: THE ART AND SOUL OF JOHN DENVER
Book/CD Pack
This songbook/CD pack is a must for John Denver fans, who will not want to miss the large color section featuring his never-before-published nature and travel photography, concert memorabilia and new interviews about his songwriting craft with the people who knew and worked with him. The 23 Denver classics include: Annie's Song • Leaving on a Jet Plane • Sunshine on My Shoulders • and more.
02500566 Piano/Vocal/Guitar $19.95

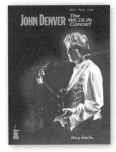

JOHN DENVER – THE WILDLIFE CONCERT
This matching folio to John Denver's second live album – a two-CD set accompanying a cable TV special and home video – features 29 fabulous tracks: Amazon • Annie's Song • Bet on the Blues • Calypso • Darcy Farrow • Eagles and Horses • Falling Out of Love • The Harder They Fall • Is It Love? • Leaving on a Jet Plane • Me and My Uncle • A Song for All Lovers • Sunshine on My Shoulders • You Say That the Battle Is Over • and more.
_____ 02500326 Piano/Vocal/Guitar $17.95

P/V/G SHEET MUSIC
02504223	**Annie's Song**	$3.95
02504181	**For You**	$3.99
02504225	**Leaving on a Jet Plane**	$3.95
02509538	**Perhaps Love**	$3.95
02504219	**Sunshine on My Shoulders**	$3.95
02504214	**Take Me Home, Country Roads**	$3.95

GUITAR BOOKS

JOHN DENVER ANTHOLOGY FOR EASY GUITAR
This superb collection of 42 great Denver songs made easy for guitar includes: Annie's Song • Leaving on a Jet Plane • Take Me Home, Country Roads • plus performance notes, a biography, and Denver's thoughts on the songs.
02506878 Easy Guitar $15.95

JOHN DENVER AUTHENTIC GUITAR STYLE
12 never-before-published acoustic guitar note-for-note transcriptions of the most popular songs by John Denver. Includes the hits: Annie's Song • Sunshine on My Shoulders • Take Me Home, Country Roads • and more.
02506901 Acoustic Guitar Transcriptions $14.95

THE BEST OF JOHN DENVER
Over 20 of Denver's best-known hits spanning his 25-year career! Includes: Annie's Song • Leaving on a Jet Plane • Rocky Mountain High • Thank God I'm a Country Boy • Sunshine on My Shoulders • and more.
02506879 Easy Guitar $9.95

JOHN DENVER COLLECTION
Strum & Sing Series
A great unplugged and pared-down collection of chords and lyrics for 40 favorite John Denver songs, including: Annie's Song • Calypso • Fly Away • Follow Me • Higher Ground • Rocky Mountain High • Take Me Home, Country Roads • This Old Guitar • and more.
02500632 Guitar/Vocal $9.95

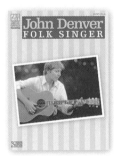

JOHN DENVER – FOLK SINGER
15 songs transcribed note for note from this country-folk entertainer and humanitarian. Includes: Fly Away • I Guess He'd Rather Be in Colorado • Mother Nature's Son • Potter's Wheel • Take Me Home, Country Roads • Thirsty Boots • This Old Guitar • Today • and more.
02500984 Play-It-Like-It-Is Guitar $19.95

JOHN DENVER – GREATEST HITS FOR FINGERSTYLE GUITAR
For the first time ever, 11 favorite Denver standards in fingerstyle arrangements that incorporate the melodies of the songs and can therefore be played as solo guitar pieces or vocal accompaniments. Includes: Annie's Song • Leaving on a Jet Plane • Rocky Mountain High • and more.
02506928 Fingerstyle Guitar $14.95

cherry lane
music company

EXCLUSIVELY DISTRIBUTED BY
HAL•LEONARD CORPORATION
7777 W. BLUEMOUND RD. P.O. BOX 13819 MILWAUKEE, WI 53213

For a complete listing of available Cherry Lane titles, please visit our web site at **www.cherrylaneprint.com**

0812